Better Business English

By H. GEORGE CLASSEN

Drawings by Herb Green

ARCO PUBLISHING COMPANY, INC.
New York

Published by ARCO PUBLISHING COMPANY, Inc.
219 Park Avenue South, New York, N.Y. 10003

Library of Congress Catalog Card Number 65-27339

Arco Catalog Number 1350

Printed in the United States of America

Contents

1
Writing in our Lives

"IN the beginning was the word. . . ."

A famous and impressive phrase, but baffling too, and open to various interpretations. Yet at the bottom of it there is a deep and abiding truth, a truth not only about the world outside and beyond ourselves, but about our inside world. It is this: Life's meaning depends on our ability to recognize different things and acts and to place them in proper sequence. But to do so we must first be able to distinguish them from one another, to classify and to label them. Unless we give things their proper name and order them in their proper sequence, we shall be lost in a world of chaos where nothing has meaning. Our phrase could therefore read: "In the beginning was meaning."

The meaning, the "word," may be transmitted from mind to mind in various ways. One of the most efficient, impressive and potent ways is writing. So potent can it be that in many cultures writing has been regarded as magic.

In our own culture, the importance of writing continues to grow, and the number of effects that can be achieved without words shrinks more and more. It is true that there are computers and other complicated pieces of machinery which use numbers or other non-verbal symbols. But anyone who has seen the proliferation of advertisements for "technical writers" will realize that these machines have done as much to swell the ranks of the word-wielders as any other innovation. There is television, of course, the great competitor of newspaper and magazine. But most words heard on television are written before they are spoken, and this does not take into account the flood of writing that goes on behind the scenes. There is the telephone, and much of the business that was formerly carried on by letter is now done by local or long-distance call; but a study of United States Government letter writing showed that during the years 1912-1953 (when telephone service had its greatest expansion) the volume of letters increased ten times faster than the number of employees. Track down any fact, any action, and chances are that some-

So potent is writing that in many cultures it has been regarded as magic

where along the line you will find that the fact or the action depends on what is written.

Some people deplore this growing power of the written word. I don't — not only because I earn my living by it (a weighty reason, to be sure), but because I believe that the abuses to which writing is prey are of the same kind as have been committed, and would be committed, in other methods of communicating meaning. There is nothing inherently good or bad about writing as such, there are only good and bad writers. And since the roots of our writing style lie buried in our psyche, it is to our psyche that we must descend if we wish to improve it.

During 1912-53 government letter writing increased ten times faster than the number of employees

That's what this book will help you to do.

It is not a psychological thriller It does not get down on your knees with you, so to speak, to dig up from the muck of your childhood nightmares the squirming little demons that bedevil your style. It isn't a learned treatise, and you will find many old, familiar words and phrases that have dogged your steps for years, sometimes like shadows. You will find that, far from being ominous, most of them are just funny, or even ridiculous. And once you have made that discovery, your writing will not be the same again. It will be better.

2
Splendid Raiment

AS YOU MAY have sensed from the preceding introduction, this book makes certain assumptions, and one of them is that you are an educated, literate person who writes, or expects to write, a good deal. It does not matter what sort of writing you do — whether you are a junior executive who is trying his hand at inter-office memos, a geologist who compiles reports on bedrock stratigraphy, a clubwoman who has to keep minutes of meetings, a civil servant who explains the latest tax law to puzzled citizens, a college student who would like to get better marks, or an ambitious journalist.

This book also assumes that you can spell, and that you can punctuate no worse than its author — which is enough to get by. I have read a great many letters, reports, essays, etc., and I have found that with most businessmen, college people, and journalists spelling is no great problem. Neither, surprisingly, is grammar, or at least that basic correctness we think of when we see the word "grammar."

Another assumption I am making (I might as well admit that it is I who is assuming all this) is that you are human; in other words, that you àre an ill-co-ordinated jumble of frailties, desires, apprehensions, phobias, ambitions, and sympathies. One of these typically human qualities, you will agree, is the wish to make a certain impression on other people,

people who can help you or hurt you, love you or despise you.
And your only means of making an impression on them is to
communicate with them.

So far, so good. Speech is a form of communication. *Written*
speech is one of the most lasting forms of communication.
The ancient Greeks have disappeared, and their civilization
has crumbled into dust. We know practically nothing of their
music or their painting, but much of what their great men
wrote is with us still, and still begets powerful new ideas and
emotions. Yes, writing is so permanent, it is such a faithful
record. It continues to communicate long after its original
purpose was served, and it is often surprising what strange
secondary purposes it may be used for, not at all foreseen by

In many ways, writing serves the same purpose as dress

the writer. It is almost as if the writer had surrendered a piece
of his own life into the possession of others.

Are you aware of this? Are you ever!

That is why you are taking care in writing, just as you are
taking care in dressing. Dress, as it happens, is a pretty important means of communication in its own right, and in many
ways it works like writing.

In the Middle Ages when few people were able to write
and fewer had occasion to do so, men had to express many
things in their apparel which we express in writing. I don't
believe anyone has ever made a study of the correlation between the spread of writing and the growing plainness of male
attire during the past several centuries. If anyone did, he might
discover that men found they no longer needed to bother with
silver buckles, lacy shirts, red velvet doublets, plumed hats,
and padded calves because they had discovered that they could
reproduce the same effects more cheaply in their writing.

This discovery, of course, was not entirely new. It had been
made long ago by those select few who did know how to
write. Consider the beginning of this letter from King Darius
of Persia to Alexander of Macedonia:

> *From the capital of the kings of the world: As long as
> the sun shines on the head of Alexander the robber, etc.,
> let him know that the King of Heaven has bestowed on
> me the dominion of the earth, and the Almighty has
> granted to me the surface of the four quarters. Providence
> has also distinguished me with glory, exaltation, majesty,
> and with multitudes of devoted champions and confed-
> erates.*
>
> *A report has reached us that you have gathered to your-
> self numbers of thieves and reprobates, the multitude of
> whom has so elated your imagination that you propose
> through their co-operation to procure the crown and
> throne, lay waste our kingdom, and destroy our land and
> people. . . . It now behooves you, on reading the contents*

*of this epistle, to return instantly from the place to which
you have advanced.*

Coarse wits may say that the entire meaning of the letter
could have been rendered more effectively by the single word,
Scram. Thoughtful readers who remember that not long after
this letter Alexander defeated Darius's armies and took possession of Persia may wonder whether Darius's boasting did
not betray a dreadful premonition.

Modern statesmen do not bluster as Darius did; they use
different words. But their statements and messages often show
a secret fear also, as do those of businessmen, students, lawyers, clubwomen, politicians, and housewives. What sort of
fear is this?

It is fear — or, if you like, apprehension — that the written message will not convey an image of the writer as an
important, influential, valuable, ethical, cultured, tasteful,
knowledgeable, sympathetic, respectful, and guiltless person.
The more you depend on writing to project the image, the
wider the scope for this fear.

When we look into it a little more closely, we find that
this seldom acknowledged but powerful feeling can be sub-
divided as follows:

We fear that the reader will —

(1) think little of us
(2) hold us responsible
(3) misconstrue our message
(4) be offended.

There is nothing mystic about this fourfold division. It suits
me; if it does not suit you, you can make a threefold or a
fivefold division. Either way it will alter neither my projected
image nor my message.

These various sub-fears our subconscious strives to placate,
by making our writing

(1) pompous
(2) hedging

(3) wordy

(4) hypocritical.

These are unpleasant terms, and if you wish to forget them, do so, by all means. One of the things I wish to avoid more than anything else is the appearance of foisting on you a formula. I have examined a good many books on better writing, and several of them, I regret to say, employ formulas, such as A-B-C-D-E, 7 C's, 4-S, and so forth. It isn't that writing is too free-wheeling and creative to be bound by dry mathematics, though there is a lot of truth in that, too. It is

The writer is haunted by a fourfold fear

simply that I do not believe that you, or anyone, will long remember formulas and, what is more, will take the trouble to apply them faithfully and diligently to each and every piece of writing.

As to my fourfold division, it is useful as an introduction to this book, and to make sure that it serves this purpose I shall keep harping on its elements for a while. By the time you get to the final chapters you will be so infused with the meaning of my message that you will not need artificial reminders.

There are a good many books on the English language available to the man who wishes to improve his writing. Any fair-sized bookstore or library will have from ten to fifty books, large and small, on everything from spelling to composition, from the business letter to the scientific essay. These books often go into painstaking detail on orthography, sentence structure, punctuation, paragraphing, and so on. They are very useful to a man who sincerely wants to learn how to write well.

The trouble is that few men really want to learn how to write well — for the sake of writing well. Before they will want to learn *how* they must learn *why*. And it is on this point that the books of the grammarians fail to persuade.

If the makers of soap, antiseptics, and toothpaste had to depend on appeals to health and cleanliness alone for their advertising pitch, their sales would probably be but a small portion of what they are. Why? Because most people put a higher priority on being loved and accepted than on being clean and healthy. That is why the soap and toothpaste makers usually aim their Sunday punch at the heart rather than the head.

This book, too, aims its pitch at your heart, and you may already have gathered what it is. It is an appeal to your manliness, in the broad sense of the word embracing both sexes. I could, of course, also say that the book will help you to stop making an ass of yourself, but that would be too negative an approach, and might merely substitute one type of fear for another. Courage, my friends, and bold precision!

Some teachers of better English, after futile attempts to penetrate the emotional barrier, reach for the axe. Their axe is the formula: Write simply. Always, at all costs. Use short words. Use short sentences. Write short paragraphs. One author professes admiration for the Chinese language, because it strings its uninflected one-syllable words together like beads.

This is not *my* way. I did not diligently and at great cost build a large vocabulary and a fertile and inventive style to throw it all overboard and to go back to writing in the manner of "Fun with Dick and Jane."

Consider the following two examples:

In general, increased aminopeptidase activity was observed in the myelocytes and mature neutrophils in chronic myelocytic leukemia as well as in the younger myelocytes in acute-subacute leukemia; myeloblasts and promyelocytes were non-reactive.

A multi-plant manufacturer has a challenging position which should be of interest to a University Graduate whose principal responsibilities will involve the development and implementation of detailed plans for the solution of complicated and divergent problems.

What is wrong with these two sentences?

There is, of course, nothing wrong with the first sentence. There is much wrong with the second.

Someone has said that for every action, for every feeling there is not more than one word in the dictionary that is exactly right, and sometimes there is not even one word. The first of our examples is from a medical report in a scientific journal, and the author, writing for specialists, uses the right words to convey precise information. The second sentence is from an advertisement for a "project analyst" (whatever that may mean) and the writer uses a flood of pompous verbiage to convey very little information, and inaccurately at that.

There is a time and place for short words, and there is a time and place for long ones. Much of what I shall have to say in the following pages may emphasize shortness and simplicity, because these qualities are the foundation of good writing. But they are not the sum and substance of it.

In my book on the history of the Canada-United States boundary (*Thrust and Counterthrust,* Longmans Canada Ltd.) I wrote that the British boundary commissioner on the 49th-parallel survey "spent the long winter evenings in lonely and dogmatic lucubration." *Webster's* defines "lucubration" as

It is no use merely to add to your knowledge of writing

"laborious study . . . elaborate literary composition . . . over-labored work," and this, together with the mournful sound of the word and its alliterative kinship with "lonely," seemed to fit perfectly the man and the mood. It is quite possible that in my writing career I shall never use that word again, but I am glad that I remembered it when it was called for.

What it all comes down to is this: It is no use merely to add to your knowledge of writing. Unless your inner self participates in the process of learning and in fact undergoes a change, your writing will not improve. The failings I am talking about are moral, not technical. The remedy is also moral. Any other approach is apt to be superficial in effect, like the favorite aphorism of a well-known comic-strip character, which goes, roughly, "Honesty is better than cheating, because it's nicer."

Man, of course, is imitative, and may even imitate manners of style that spring from insecurity, even though the imitator himself may be perfectly secure and fearless. Unfortunately, style not only springs from character, it also affects character. It works both ways. Thus, even if you are without fear or failing, this book is useful for you, because it will help you not only to be fearless, but also to appear fearless.

3

The Overloaded Donkey

HOW DO pomposity, hedging, wordiness, and hypocrisy work out in practice?

Pomposity, caused by our subconscious desire to appear important, expresses itself in large, abstract words, words that have an independent impact, that stand out like obelisks in a desert, arresting the viewer's gaze. They are not intended to help along the basic message, they are there solely to proclaim the writer's importance by their own bigness.

Years ago, when it was still possible to joke about the atomic bomb, a cartoon appeared in a popular magazine: An Indian on a New Mexico mesa is squatting before a small camp fire, over which he is waving a blanket, sending up smoke signals. While he is thus engaged an atomic bomb explodes somewhere in the distance, raising a mushroom cloud. The Indian stares at the huge bomb cloud, and murmurs enviously, "Gee, wish I'd said that!"

I don't know anything about smoke signals, but I doubt that a single puff of smoke, however gigantic, could possibly "say" anything. But we laugh at the joke because we are so accustomed to mistaking bigness for meaning.

In darkest New Guinea there is said to dwell a tribe which uses tom-tom signals to communicate from village to village. They never managed to develop a code of any sort, however,

20

and when they have something to tell they just beat their hollow logs like mad. The infernal racket tells the other villages that something important has happened and that they had better get excited. Some business communications are like that.

If you think I'm exaggerating, consider the following sentence from a statement by a very high-ranking Canadian government official about the future of the northern territories:

Here then is as unexciting an assessment as it seems to me possible to provide on the economic possibilities of

Something important has happened ... but what?

the North. On the basis of conditions as they now look
— and recognizing all the problems — it seems to me
that it would be the course of the most extreme unwis-
dom for us not to make a fairly substantial investment
of intelligence, imagination, effort and money in trying
to make possible the sort of development that seems
capable of realization.

But "possible" and "capable of realization" mean exactly
the same thing. In a big mouthful of words, not a grain of
meaning.

A common excuse for this sort of thing is that the writer,
or speaker, did not have time to produce a more polished
composition, that he has been out of school many a long year,
and that English just isn't being taught any more as it used
to be and as it should be.

This may all be true, but it still skirts the main issue. I have
watched bureaucrats and scientists as they mull over their
reports, memoranda, and speech drafts, and they do not
usually look like people in a hurry. It takes loving care to
produce sentences such as: "Your mineral sample has been
subjected to visual observation." The school alibi does not
explain this, either. I have a teen-aged son in school, and
when he watches the girls go by he does not say that he is
subjecting them to visual observation.

I don't wish to imply that everything is all right with the
teaching of English, and that our high-school and college students are masters of style. But their failings are mostly innocent
failings. If they express themselves badly it is because they
don't try hard enough to measure up to the standards set by
their teachers. But the stylistic faults of modern businessmen
or scientists are rarely so innocent. They fail to write well
because they are trying too hard — to measure up to a standard that cannot be found in any style book.

(You may be impatient to find out exactly what it is that
makes an expression or a phrase pompous. Relax; you will
not have to wait much longer.)

Consider hedging. Hedging, dissembling, evasive writing arises from a desire not to be held responsible for unpopular, controversial, or potentially erroneous statements. The writer who hedges seeks to dissociate his own person from the action he describes or advocates. He seeks to phrase his statements in such a way that he cannot be put on the spot. He operates with double meanings and conditional clauses.

It seems odd that pomposity and hedging, two apparently opposite qualities, should so often occur together in modern writing. But to crave power without responsibility is a familiar human failing, to which we are all more or less susceptible.

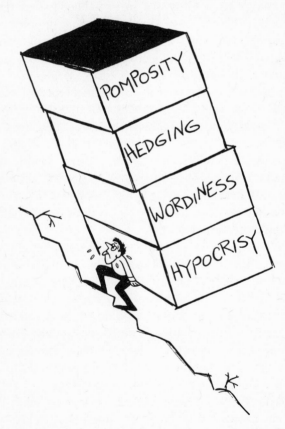

Some writers overload their messages with extra burdens

Wordiness shows up as repetition, the needless piling-on of words that are mere variations of something said previously. It often stems from the writer's insecurity about his own capacity to express himself clearly. This lack of faith in oneself often leads to lack of faith in the intelligence or education of the prospective reader — a hint that few readers will take kindly. Wordiness thus tends to achieve an effect opposite to that which it is meant to serve. It beclouds the issue instead of clarifying it. Since this is close to the purpose of hedging, it is often difficult for an editor to decide whether he is dealing with a case of deliberate hedging or mere wordiness, or both.

Wordiness may also spring from a mistaken desire to be polite. Many letter writers believe that it is impolite to write a letter of only one paragraph, and they spin out what they have to say to two or three paragraphs, even if this means that they have to say the same thing over again in different words. It is true that excessive brevity carries with it a sense of brusqueness which may offend many people. A one-line letter cannot but look ridiculous. But it is easy enough to be both brief and pleasant, avoiding both wordiness and brusqueness.

This touches on the fourth failing in my catalog of writer's fears — hypocrisy, or false friendliness and flattery. It is difficult to introduce an insincere and fulsome tone into a piece of writing that comes straight to the point, but a pompous, hedging, wordy style almost seems to demand it. And no wonder — if it were not laced with some artificial sweeteners, such a style would be well-nigh intolerable.

A piece of writing that has to embody all these overtones and undertones is indeed a multi-purpose vehicle. Since some of these overtones and undertones are disharmonious, it might also be described as a cross-purpose vehicle.

Government officials have often been accused of being especially prone to such stylistic excesses, but in my experience they are by no means the worst offenders. One of the richest hunting grounds for inflated, insincere prose is the display advertisements for engineers, sales managers, data-processing specialists and the like published in large newspapers, such as the *New York Times* and, in Canada, the *Financial Post*. Almost equally rewarding to the seeker of bad examples are annual reports to shareholders and club literature. This is probably because the men and women who compose these statements strive so desperately to create an impression without giving too much information.

The cumulative effect of a fear-placating style is to burden down your writing. There is a German saying that a gold-laden donkey will jump over the highest fence. (Meaning: an unscrupulous politician will disregard any principle, if the payoff is large enough.) But the burden you place on your writing when you are fearful about your image is not gold.

Or let us look at it this way. There is the message, the rea-

With some writers, the accompaniment drowns out the melody

son for your writing. And there are the extra devices, the ornaments, added to convey an image of the writer. The two elements can be compared to the melody and the accompaniment in music. You know that in piano music, for example, it is generally the highest note played with the right hand that has the tune, the lower notes, played with the left hand, carrying the accompaniment. Some composers, to add spice and variation to their music, will occasionally cause the melody to dip into the bass while the accompaniment runs over into the high notes. This makes the piano player play cross-handed, and if he is skillful he can still make the melody come through.

Some writers seem to set all their music for cross-handed playing — their accompaniment is more obvious than their melody.

With these broad principles properly digested, we should now be in the right frame of mind to look at specifics.

4

Demon Noun...

LET US take another look at the advertisement for a "project analyst" in Chapter 2. If we break it down by parts of speech we find that it contains no fewer than ten nouns (eleven, if we count the adjectival "University"). The excess of nouns is not the only thing wrong with the sample, but it is an important fault. It is the chief characteristic of the pompous writer. The pompous writer uses adjectives and adverbs sparingly, verbs only as a last resort, but with nouns he is lavish.

In the Talmud there is a story about a famous rabbi. This rabbi was stopped by a Gentile who said jokingly, "I have heard a lot about you. I don't want to be bothered with tiresome explanations, but I'll become a convert to Judaism if you can explain to me the whole of your Law while I'm standing on one leg." The rabbi replied: "Do unto others as you would have others do unto you. That is the whole Law; the rest is commentary."

If I were placed in a position similar to that of the rabbi, I would say: "The fewer nouns the better — that is the gist of my message; the rest is commentary."

The noun is the biggest word of all; it represents a thing. In German, as you may know, all nouns are capitalized; this is sometimes taken as evidence that Germans are by nature pompous. (The Germans counter by pointing out that Anglo-

Demon Noun

Saxons alone of all peoples capitalize the first personal pronoun; this is supposed to be evidence that the British are
egocentric.)

But people with a predilection for nouns do not think of
all this. They simply feel it in their bones that nouns will
increase their stature in the eyes of the reader. Therefore they
convert other words and phrases into nouns. They do this by
robbing all other parts of speech of their vitality, reducing
them to a purely ancillary role. Compare the following:

to refer	to make reference
to correct	to take corrective action
to help	to be of assistance
to receive	to be in receipt of
to consider	to have under consideration

There is no difference in meaning between the left and right columns. But the words in the left column are clear and agreeable to read; those in the right column are slightly fuzzy and therefore annoying.

But the pompous writer will instinctively plump for the right column when choosing his expressions. This is easy to test. Pick up a scientific report, an office memorandum, a club circular, or whatever else is handy (preferably from your own pen) and try to convert as many nouns as you can into verbs. Do you feel little jabs of pain just below your diaphragm? That is your pompous little ego twitching.

Verbs are not the only words that are turned into nouns for the sake of pomposity. Prepositions, adjectives, conjunctions, adverbs are also turned into nouns.

important	of importance
because	in view of, as a result of
now	at the present time
soon	at an early date
more than	in excess of
that	the fact that
most	the majority of
mainly	in the main
for	for the purpose of

and so on, almost ad infinitum. It is not necessary to know the grammatical terms of the words that are sacrificed in favor of nouns. It is necessary only to recognize the superfluous noun, and to eliminate it. Once you have become alert to it you will spot it almost automatically and without extra effort. Anyone with a fair grasp of the English language can convert

It is of great importance that action be taken in respect of this matter at the earliest possible date

into

It is very important that something be done about this matter as soon as possible.

By making such a conversion you will often gain a bonus in clarity. In the preceding example, "action" suggests that a definite remedy has already been decided on, even though this may not be so. But "something" is embarrassingly frank. (We shall take up this question a little later.)

Noun-addiction is often found where one would least expect it — among efficiency and communications experts. A report on United States Government correspondence says:

> *Each agency handling large volumes of letters shall make provision for correspondence management on a continuing staff basis.*

This sentence ought to read:
> *Each agency handling large volumes of letters shall provide for correspondence management with continuing staff.*

Another expert on language and letters, announcing a series of training courses, said:

> *Management has made arrangements for the continuance of this series for a period of three months, provided that a sufficient number of employees indicate their willingness to participate.*

Which converts to:
> *Management has arranged that this series may continue for three months, provided that enough employees indicate that they are willing to participate.*

And, if we wish to reap the clarity bonus as well, we can further reduce that last part of the sentence to read "provided that enough employees sign up."

An instructress in letter writing was so smitten with this course that she said, "It makes one realize how little he understands about a skill he practices every day." To which we can only reply, *Touché!*

A mining company report says:

> *During the year the laboratory further investigated the use of bacteria for the leaching of uranium ores which has potential for process cost reductions.*

This sentence becomes a lot clearer, and less pompous, if we knock out a few nouns:

> *During the year the laboratory further investigated the use of bacteria for leaching uranium ores, which may reduce processing costs.*

The courageous writer cuts nouns down to size

In the report of a traffic-safety council we find this sentence:
While we are unable to pinpoint statistically the fact that mechanical failure causes accidents, there is a growing belief that this is definitely contributory.

Well, as they say, a fact is a fact is a fact. What the safety expert really wanted to say, I assume, was:
Although we cannot prove statistically that mechanical failure causes accidents, the belief is growing that it contributes to them.

Had he put his sentence in these simple terms, the writer would probably have realized that it was an inaccurate or at least inadequate statement. We need no elaborate statistics to prove that *some* accidents are caused by mechanical failure alone. The writer would have been compelled to be more exact. As it is, he told us nothing meaningful at all.

The same applies to the budget director who defined "short-term projects" as follows:

Short-term projects are those that have an expectancy of termination within a term of months or years depending on the support given.

Had he eliminated the unnecessary nouns — "expectancy," "termination," "term," — he might have seen that projects continuing for years cannot be called short-term. What lasts longer than "years"?

Is there anything the pompous writer likes better than a noun? Yes: two nouns. The pompous journalist has long since given up reporting that unions vote in favor of striking; they now vote in favor of "strike action." Nor are airplanes grounded nowadays by bad weather; they succumb only to bad "weather conditions." The words "action" and "condition" add nothing to the meaning. They are there only to impress. "The purpose of this memorandum is to remind you" means simply "This is to remind you." It is evident to the reader that what he has before him is a memorandum.

That would seem to be all there is to the question of unnecessary nouns. But one cannot dally with Demon Noun without being burned by his hot breath. I alluded to this when I spoke of the clarity bonus. Who of us, for example, has not abused the word "basis"? We have already met it in our example about correspondence management. In a sentence such as "Meetings of the club are suspended on a temporary basis,"

The pompous weatherman predicts rainy weather conditions

the word is used merely to displace an adverb ("temporarily"), but many writers do not stop there. When they write, "The men are being paid on a weekly basis," do they mean that the men are being paid every week, or that their pay is computed by the week rather than by the hour or by the day? People working for the government, for example, are paid on an annual basis — their salaries are quoted by the year. This does not mean that they are paid only once a year.

The confusion is just as great when "basis" is used in a

phrase where it could also mean a physical foundation: "The tent is to be put up on a permanent basis." Does this mean that the tent itself is to be permanent, or that only the foundation is permanent?

In pursuit of pomposity we have actually flushed out two other symptoms of fear — hedging and wordiness. The man who needlessly adds "basis" to his adverbs may actually delude himself into believing that he has made his meaning clearer. We have seen that the opposite is true. But he may also wish to obscure his meaning, to escape responsibility for a potentially erroneous or unpopular statement.

It may well be, for example, that the company director who writes that "wage increases were instituted," merely wishes to sound important. But it may also be that this phrase seems to him less painful for the shareholders, and more flattering for the workers, than the straightforward "wages were increased."

These examples show that several symptoms of fear may occur together — a phenomenon whose ramifications will quickly become apparent.

5

...and Other Demons

I HAVE KNOWN a scientist who seemed incapable of writing the word "research" without tacking on the word "program." On the face of it this appears to be nothing more than an innocuous case of pomposity, two nouns being better than one. But it is a little more than that. "Program," after all, does suggest the existence of a plan, a development having a beginning and a foreseeable end.

But my scientist used "program" in situations where it could not possibly mean a plan. He would write:

The adherence on the part of all technicians to adequate safety precautions is of vital importance for the research program of this department.

Evidently he was referring to the work as such, without having in mind any specific plan, project, or task. By this indiscriminate use he robbed the word of all meaning, since it became impossible to tell when he was referring to a specific plan, and when not. Perhaps there lurked in the back of his mind a desire to give the impression that his department had a plan for everything, including its own dissolution. More likely, though, he was plagued by a hidden fear that if he failed to say "research *program*" he would not make himself clear.

This type of fear, as I said earlier, finds its expression in
wordiness. The editorialist who writes that Mr. So-and-so has
done more for local schools "than any one man," probably
fears that if he left out "one" the readers would think of more
than one man, although it is difficult to see how "any man"
could be more than one. The geologist who reports that the
rock crystals are "larger in size than those found previously,"
and the geographer who tells us that "the hills in this area are

The wordy writer is lavish with extra nouns

of lower height than those farther south," may believe that the
deletion of "size" and "height" will leave their text open to
fateful misinterpretations, though here again the reader cannot escape the uncomfortable feeling that his intelligence is
being impugned.

Bureaucrats have been known to write "Enclosed herewith
please find attached," even though anything that is attached to
a letter must perforce be enclosed with it. Words such as

"area," "field," "phase," and "function" are often found strewn about in modern reports and memoranda with such abandon that every vestige of clarity and precision vanishes. When an expert on municipal finance speaks of "expenditures in the social welfare area of this municipality," does he refer to a slum, or does he mean social welfare as a municipal department?

Reporting to his shareholders, a company president wrote:

The competitive situation which prevailed throughout the world during the preceding year was intensified in 19 . ., particularly in the areas of market prices and quality standards. Although sales increased satisfactorily and record tonnages were produced, this competition together with rising manufacturing costs, resulted in reduced profit margins. Every effort has been made to improve the situation by increasing efficiencies, curtailing costs and directing marketing action to the most rewarding product areas. . . . Increasingly severe competition was again the predominant feature in international marketing areas.

The word "area" in this verbose quotation is apparently being used in three ways. In the first instance it seems to mean "category," in the second, "line," and in the third "region." This cannot but confuse the reader. Yet "area" (or its equivalent) is superfluous in all three cases. With the deletion of a few other extra nouns (how do you intensify a situation, anyway?), and without striving for stylistic perfection, the quotation could be made to read:

The competition which prevailed throughout the world during the preceding year became more intense in 19 . ., particularly concerning prices and quality. Although sales increased satisfactorily and record quantities were produced, this competition together with rising manufacturing costs decreased profits. Strenuous efforts were made to improve the situation by increasing efficiency, lowering costs, and emphasizing the marketing of the most profitable lines. . . . Increasingly severe competition was again the predominant feature in international markets.

A scientist is recommended for higher salary because he "exercises a management function," which fails to make clear whether he is a full-time manager, a part-time manager, or whether he exercises only one of the various functions normally expected of a manager.

Wordy explorer investigates the temperature characteristics of sea ice

Administrators have an obligation to acquire a degree of
familiarity with the research phase of this organization,
a head of a company wrote in a circular letter. This suggests
that the organization, during its development, had to pass
through several phases like a growing youngster, and that one
of these was research. This was not so: the organization was
devoted entirely to research, from start to finish.

A manual on organization tells us that most forecasting
techniques are "mathematical in nature," which is two words
too many, and an arctic explorer wordily investigates the
"temperature characteristics" of the sea ice. We have already.
met "profit margins," which are not necessarily the same as
"profits." A personnel director wrote:

The company has on its payroll a total of 5,684 em-
ployees, of which 1,793 are in the salaried and 3,891 in
the hourly-rated groups.

We'll pass over the wrong application of "which" to people,
and point out only that "payroll" is redundant — where else
would company employees be? — as are "total" and "groups."

A miner in northern Ontario who had recently arrived
from the United States got a circular letter from a mill in the
same region saying that the mill would close down for "the
winter months." The American, to whom "the winter months"
meant December, January, and February, waited until mid-
November to take his first truckload of ore to the mill. The
mill was closed. The mill manager, a wordy writer, was in the
habit of tacking on "months" whenever he mentioned one of
the four seasons. He did not actually intend to refer to any
particular months. "Winter months" to him meant the same
as "winter," except that it seemed to sound more exact and
businesslike. Had he merely written "winter," the miner might
have taken the trouble to inquire how long the winter lasted
in the area. (It lasts from October to April, inclusive.)

Definitions of time generally bring out wordiness in the
insecure writer. He will insist on talking about "the month of

January," even though January has never been anything but a month. "Early summer" becomes "the early part of summer," "the present" becomes "the present time," and "the fall" becomes "the fall season." The short and exact word "now" is avoided by the pompous writer as if it were a sign of bad taste. Its replacement by "at present" or "currently" is not particularly objectionable, even if one writer, not being satisfied with "currently," made it "concurrently," which is a horse of a different color. I think I should faint from surprise if I heard a master of ceremonies introduce an after-dinner speaker with words other than "At this time, it is my pleasure. . . ."

But when "now" is displaced in favor of "as of now," we have reason to become suspicious. When a building super-

Winter and winter months are not necessarily identical

intendent writes, "As of now, students will no longer be permitted to use the freight elevator," we conclude that it means "from now on." But when a press release by the air force says, "As of now, there are no plans for bombing raids beyond the former demarcation line," does this mean "from now on" or "at the moment"?

It is, of course, always possible that the fuzziness of such statements is deliberate, i.e., that the writer wishes to hedge. This point will be taken up in the next chapter.

The fear of omitting an essential phrase, a word, a classification, of failing to cover all conceivable aspects of some subject is the chief cause of logorrhea, the whimsical Greek compound meaning an uncontrollable stream of words. In a manual for supervisors in the Canadian civil service we read:

> *The sense in which we use the word "supervisor" in this course applies to any person who directs the work of others, or who directs the work that these others perform.*

It is impossible to see any difference between "the work of others" and "the work that these others perform." Another definition in this manual says:

> *Objectives are goals established to guide the endeavors of the organization. . . . The objectives and goals of an organization set its course, and management must know these goals and objectives thoroughly.*

But if objectives *are* goals, the second sentence actually refers to "the goals and goals of an organization," which is absurd.

Some writers are so imbued with the importance of certain words that they would rather risk using them once too often than not enough:

> *We are not able to take this man on our staff because his eyesight does not meet the usual requirements which are required for this position.*

*The responsibility for authorizing travel, directly con-
nected with the operating program of the Department, is
the responsibility of the Branch Directors.*

We may ask only in passing in what sense "operating program" is preferable to "operations."

Others, apparently accustomed to dealing with amorphous
masses of humanity, cannot refer to actual people without
some fuss:

*Individual members desiring to participate in the tour
may do so by leaving their names and telephone numbers
with the Club Secretary.*

How *non*-individual members may leave their names and
telephone numbers is a bit of a mystery. Perhaps the writer was
thinking of phantoms — persons of flesh and blood cannot
tour via telephone, anyway.

Here is a fine example of all-round wordiness, in a letter
from the head of a government laboratory to a company
director:

*I can assure you that we do not intend to let you down
in regard to anything that we can do here toward render-
ing assistance to your company in firmly establishing its
important industry. There is indeed a lot to be done and
our facilities and staff will be available to tackle the
problems which require solution.*

And here is another, culled from — of all things — a Pen-
tagon memorandum ordering a purge of the language of the
Defense Department:

*I am forming a task force to review attitudes, methods,
and types including written, telephone, as well as person-
to-person contacts of responses being made to the public
by all components of DoD within the Washington area
and world wide.*

It is surprising how the addition of one or two needless nouns may encumber a simple sentence by altering its structure:

Reduction of the ore may be carried out either by a single-stage or a two-stage process.

If we delete "process" and turn "reduction" into the verb it should be, we get:

The ore may be reduced in one or two stages.

Finally, there are the wordsmiths, the men who view all uncompounded and unmodified words with deep feelings of inadequacy. They will say that two problems are "interrelated," apparently fearing that if they used the word "related" the reader might think the problems were not related to one another. Yet they quite naturally say that "Mary, John, and Louise are related," and have no such misgivings. From this rather innocent construction they advance to bolder terms, such as the "uniquely rare" experience. "Unique" means one of its kind, and "uniquely rare" is therefore a contradiction in terms, since "rare" means few of its kind. In the opposite category are the two pearl earrings which, we are told in great earnest, are "identically the same." One of these two terms would be just fine; together they are absurd. Absurd also is the word "irregardless."

Pomposity also plays a part here, since long and complicated words have much the same impact as extra nouns. Such words as "implement," "activate," "finalize," "encounter," "initiate," "prior to," "subsequent to," and a host of others are used to enhance images. Being especially easy to spot, these questionable baubles need no further emphasis here.

There is one word, however, for which I should like to break a lance — "anticipate."

"Anticipate" is unique, i.e., there is no close synonym for it. It means "to preclude or prevent by prior action, to fore-

stall, to experience beforehand, to foresee and do beforehand."
We may say, for instance, that a general anticipated an enemy
attack by a tactical withdrawal, that the waiter anticipated our
wish and brought us coffee before we asked for it, and the
popular old song speaks of the "keen anticipation" of a senti-
mental journey.

But, alas, this is not the sense in which the word is used
in at least nine out of ten cases. When a club treasurer writes
that "the deficit is unfortunately higher than was anticipated,"
he means, simply, that it is higher than expected. Why does
he not write "expected"? Because "anticipated" is a fancier
word, that's why. The deficit is there, all right, but who is going
to lift a hand against a man whose pen commands such pompous prose?

6

Meet the Hedgehog

IF the previous chapter may have given you some startling new slants on your own style, you are due for an even more satisfying catharsis in this one. Wordiness may be disagreeable but sometimes excusable; hedging is not.

Theoretically, hedging falls into two categories — offensive and defensive, just as a military unit may throw up a smoke screen to mask either an attack or a withdrawal. In practice, the two categories are hard to distinguish, and I shall not try to make such a distinction here. Stylistic faults that spring from moral causes are often extraordinarily hard to classify, and an expression or a paragraph which I might consider a classic case of hedging another critic would put down as mere wordiness, while a third would say that it was mainly pompous. Yet it might serve all three purposes.

Indications of this have already cropped up in the preceding pages, and it will become clearer as we progress. Take, for example, the expression "as of now." I pointed out that it is a wordy way of defining the present and may be used simply instead of "now." It may also be used for "from now on" or "until now." I also used the example "As of now, there are no plans for bombing raids." Does this mean that there are no plans now, or from now on? Or is there yet a third possibility? This question is even more apt when we read:

45

*A defense department spokesman announced today there
is no present intention of troop withdrawals from Europe.*

If this were meant as a straightforward statement, the word
"present" would be plainly superfluous: the sentence being in
the present tense, the intention, too, must necessarily be in the
present. Why, then, would a spokesman wish to overemphasize
this by the word "present"? We can conclude only that he
wishes to be free to have an intention in the future. But since
we cannot live or think in the future, this can mean only that
"there may be a present intention to have a future intention."
This is absurd. No matter how you slice it, it's doubletalk; or,
as an Indian might put it, "White man talk with forked
tongue."

This seems to be offensive hedging, leaving a loophole for
attack, without appearing to do so. An example of defensive
hedging is this sentence found in a company report:

The laboratory function has been strengthened.

This, in my experience, may mean any (or none) of the
following: (a) the staff of the laboratory has been increased,
(b) the budget of the laboratory has been increased, (c) the
laboratory has been enlarged, (d) the laboratory has been
given some new equipment, (e) more of the company's products are to be tested in the laboratory, (f) more of the laboratory's recommendations are being followed, (g) the laboratory
staff has been given a series of pep talks, (h) the chief of the
laboratory has had his title changed to vice-president in charge
of research, (i) the chief of the laboratory has been invited
to sit in on vice-presidential conferences. The purpose of such
an important-looking but exceedingly hazy formulation is to
impress the customer or the shareholder without committing
management to any specific action.

It is the supreme aim and desire of the true hedgehog never
to be caught on a limb. This, in turn, leads to his first safety
rule: Never be specific. Here is an excerpt from a letter whose

The laboratory function has been strengthened

writer complained about a defect in the construction of a geo-physical observatory:

It is apparent that the contractor supplied an inefficient workmanship in regard to the weather sealing, as shown on detail #3, drawing A-5, your plan file 182, for this project. This inefficiency is very detrimental to the sensitive instruments, as birds and insects are entering the instrument room that way.

You may have guessed it — the contractor left a hole. But

this must remain a mere inference drawn from the last part of the excerpt. To confirm it the reader would have to have access to detail #3, drawing A-5, plan file 182, i.e., to material which the writer did not sign and for which he is not demonstrably responsible.

The question naturally arises how wordiness, which springs from the fear of being misunderstood or of leaving out some essential detail, can be compatible with hedging, which seems to pursue opposite ends. Since these two failings do occur together, we are led to conclude that, while the wordy and hedging writer takes care that no *unfavorable* interpretation may be placed on his writing, he also sees to it that it is open to several *favorable* ones. In whatever ways we might interpret the "strengthening" of the "laboratory function" in the earlier example, they are all bound to enhance the image of the company.

The same writer who used the expression "inefficient workmanship" to mean "hole" also wrote the following:

> *As has been discussed recently, repairs to the Observatory Dome are of prime importance. While the date November 1 has been suggested as the earliest date for commencement of repairs it cannot be too highly emphasized that in view of the weather after that date, it should be started with the commencement date of November 1 in mind.*

This is really a beauty, hedgingwise, as an advertising man might say. First we are impressed with the discussions, while being carefully left in the dark as to the participants. In the second sentence, when we ask what should be started, we can come up only with "commencement." As to the date on which the commencement should commence, we could no more hope to seize upon it than on the greased pig at a country fair. Do we start on November 1, or may we start on some other date while keeping November 1 "in mind"?

It is apparent that the writer is trying to have the best of two worlds. If the observatory people complain that he is not pushing the contractor hard enough, he can point to the portentous language of his letter. If the overworked contractor complains about unreasonable requests, he can be mollified by the assurance that November 1 was never specifically insisted on.

The opening words of the preceding quotation deserve a little more attention. We saw that the writer was careful not to mention who had held the discussion. It may have been the

It is the supreme aim and desire of the true
hedgehog never to be caught out on a limb

writer and the contractor, and then again it may not. This reluctance to identify oneself is almost endemic in bureaucratic circles. "It will be appreciated" is the starting phrase of millions of letters. Why not "I would appreciate"?

Faced with this question, the executive leans back, expands the executive chest, and, sighing mournfully but authoritatively, allows that modesty forbids it.

Modesty apparently also forbids the use of the second personal pronoun, as in this sally:

It is pointed out it must be realized that this practice cannot continue. It should also be borne in mind. . . .

Here "it" stands for both "I" and "you" — at least it seems that way. Is this really modesty, or is it some less admirable quality? Is it possible that the writer wishes to cover his tracks? Here is another example of the same type:

> *At this time it is desired to impress upon you the seriousness of this irregularity and it is hoped that in future all registered items forwarded from your office are recorded on a registered letter bill.*

Not only is "it" substituted for "I" or "we," but the question who exactly is to do the recording is nicely left open; and as if this were not hazy enough, the verb is also put in the wrong tense.

Hedging writers are often equally reluctant to identify third parties:

> *One group of geological survey activities investigates the geological architecture of the country.*

"Activities" do nothing; it is people who investigate.

Even misdoers benefit from the hedgehog's far-flung veils. In a pamphlet on automobile traffic safety the drinking driver is dealt with as follows:

> *The issuance of driver's licenses is a privilege and not a right. One qualification should be an agreement to undergo chemical tests when requested by the proper authority. Again accident statistics show that in a socially unacceptable number of accidents admission of alcoholic intake is made even though the driver may not appear to be drunk.*

We shall pass over the question whether it is the issuance or the receipt of the license that is a privilege. But why not spell out who is to agree to "chemical tests"? And while we are at it, we might as well spell out these tests in layman's language. And what is all this mumbo-jumbo about socially unacceptable "alcoholic intake" by who knows whom?

Hand in hand with the use of "it" instead of "I" or "we" goes the use of passive instead of active verbs.

In this section, applications for unemployment assistance are processed.

That's passive; converted to the active voice it becomes:

This section processes applications for unemployment assistance.

Whenever possible, we ought to say who does what, rather than what is being done where.

One of the hedgehog's favorite words is "limited." He loves to write that the funds at his disposal are "limited." When you look at it closely, this does not commit him to a thing: funds are never unlimited. Whatever this man does always fills "a real need," as if you could fill unreal needs. Then there is "condition." By itself the word is innocent enough. But what of "heart condition"? Is not everyone's heart in some sort of condition, good, bad, or indifferent? And whom are we trying to fool anyway when we talk of a heart condition instead of a heart ailment?

The words "responsible" and "responsibility" have been so misused and diluted that they may soon be useless to the careful writer. Strictly speaking "responsible" means answerable or accountable, and it is plain that only rational beings can be held responsible for their actions. Therefore, when a journalist writes that "torrential rains were responsible for wide-spread flooding," he is misusing the word. Animals and natural phenomena are not responsible for anything; they merely cause things. This, however, is not a very serious misuse, since it will hardly lead anyone to confuse people and rain.

But even people are not responsible for everything they do;

on the other hand, they may be responsible for things they do *not* do. Executive officers are often responsible for everything done by their staff, whether they are aware of it or not. A foreman of a group of ditch-diggers is responsible for the digging of the ditch in a certain time and according to a certain plan. He does not have to dig that ditch himself, however. This is done by the diggers, who are not responsible for the ditch. They have a duty to dig it as the foreman directs.

This may all seem pretty elementary, but it needs emphasizing, because hedging writers have taken to writing phrases such as "the responsibilities of the job will involve . . ." after which they proceed to enumerate, indiscriminately, true responsibilities and mere duties.

Given this attitude, it is little wonder that the cloudy writer is inclined to weaken every chain of cause and effect, so as to leave himself free to adduce additional causes should he be challenged on the ones he named. A mining executive reported as follows on the closing of a uranium mine:

> *Profit from the M. uranium operation was reduced sharply as a result of the cessation of mining in June, coincidental with the termination of the government stock-pile contract.*

It takes something of an expert in uranium markets to know that the cessation of mining and the termination of the government contract were not just "coincidental" — one was the cause of the other.

Here we have at last entered the heart of the hedgehog territory. It is marked not only by odd gaps and fuzzy spots in the cause-and-effect chain, but above all by a determination never to tackle any problem directly. Like the naughty school boy who deals out sly sidekicks while staring fixedly ahead and trying to appear unconcerned, the hedging writer is the devotee of the glancing blow, the hit-and-run strike. Like the Hollywood Indian, he gallops around the periphery of the wagon train, whooping and shooting feathered arrows from afar. Here is a classic example:

It is greatly regretted that the construction of the afore-
mentioned buildings cannot be completed as anticipated,
but as has been pointed out previously the current steel
strike has severely affected the availablity of several type
girders.

As it happened, the supply of "type girders" had not just
been "affected," it had been cut off. To say so directly, however, would have been in shockingly bad taste in hedgehog
land.

The roundabout approach is illustrated by the following
sentence from a scientific paper:

Investigations into the possibility of using various types
of airborne sensors to be used as an aid in geological
mapping and prospecting are tested.

No, I did not make this up — it's a genuine quote, word
for word. First of all, the action, the verb, is postponed as
long as possible, to the very end. And what is it that is being
tested? Investigations, that's what. In other words, tests are
tested. But not really investigations, but investigations of
possibilities. What possibilities? Possibilities of using airborne
sensors. For what? For using them, of course. We are testing
investigations of possibilities of the use of using them. And
so it goes — another glorious chase around the wagon train.

In a business periodical we read that modern air terminals
cost an awful lot to build and maintain, and that the airlines
have begun to complain to the cities about having to pay most
of the cost of building and maintaining them. The writer
continues:

Should the community which obviously reaps benefits
from the economic stimulation of an international airport,
be asked to share in the cost? The airlines feel this is a
factor that must be faced.

The use of "feel" instead of "think" or "believe" is itself a sign of hedging, but here it is a minor one. It is the facing of the factor that puzzles us. Apparently it means to be clearly aware of some aspect or situation. But the writer has already told us that airlines and communities are aware of it. Our

The hedging writer circles his object as the moth circles the light

guess therefore is that what the second sentence really means is: "The airlines think it should."

Another hazy expert on airplanes and airports wrote that "an improvement may soon have to be effected to the length of the runway." A little digging in the article showed that he meant the runway would have to be lengthened.

Some information is given in such cryptic brevity that it takes two or three readings and a bit of bookkeeping know-how to decipher the meaning:

Both profit margins and railway expenses will be adversely affected by the recent wage increases.

What this meant was that wage increases granted to railway employees would *increase* the company's shipping costs and consequently *decrease* its profits. To be "adversely affected" evidently may mean both to increase and to decrease, depending on the interpretation.

The hedgehog has a whole arsenal of handy words and phrases that permit him to avoid calling a spade a spade. One of them is "involve." There is a significant difference between being involved in a fight and starting one; but to the hedgehog it is all the same. A report on a new molybdenum lubricant says:

Because viscosity is not involved, the material's lubricating properties are effective over a wide range of temperatures.

What this engineer really meant to say — or what he should have said — is:

Not being viscous, the material retains its lubricating properties at widely differing temperatures.

Officials will say that the construction of a new school "involves" the expenditure of $450,000, when it *requires* the expenditure. By admitting merely that the $450,000 is somewhere in the picture they are attempting to hedge against the possibility that the construction may require other things, as yet unthought of.

Another word of the same type is "relate." A scientist returning from a field trip was told to file information with head office, in the following words:

This explanation should relate to the number of personnel in the party, time spent in the field, cost of transportation to and from the field.

The word that ought to have been used instead of "relate" is "give." Perhaps the writer wished to hedge both against the possibility that the scientist might not have the exact information requested, and against the possibility that his own superior would be angry if the writer did not demand it.

Other expressions to obscure meanings are "in connection with" and "represent." The head of a branch office is told that a man from head office will soon visit him "in connection with shortages" recently discovered in the branch office's books. The purpose of the visit, presumably, is to investigate the shortages. The branch head would probably be less disturbed by the exact word than by the vague reference. "This represents a change of policy" should most likely read "This is a change in policy."

The use of "indicate" is equally open to challenge. Generally it means "to hint" or "to intimate." But foggy writers use it to mean "to show."

This article indicates that the poor crop was due mainly to a previously unsuspected plant disease.

Does the article merely hint at this cause, or does it provide proof? It's important to know. We also learn that there is "every indication" that China will send in troops if such and such a contingency arises. Exactly how many indications, or intimations, must there be before we are justified in saying this? Things get even fuzzier when we read:

The situation is now approaching the stage where restrictive measures are indicated.

Presumably, "indicate" here stands for "necessary," but perhaps it only means "worth considering."

This chapter does not pretend to describe all of the common devices for diluting or obscuring meaning. There still remain such words as "reconsider" and many others, but I believe that by now the reader ought to have learned how to recognize and deal with such devices on his own.

In the meantime, let us proceed to the fourth failing in our quadruplet of fears — insincerity.

7

Flattery with a Capital F

THERE IS one thing, among others, which ought to have become clear from the examples of pompous, wordy, and hedging style given in the preceding chapters: bad writing habits are not confined to particular professions. This may surprise you. Having been exposed to the cult of the men in the white coats surrounded by the mysterious paraphernalia of their craft — microscopes, test tubes, computers, rockets, cyclotrons and what have you — and the aura of rigorous logic and precision which they convey, you may have been inclined to exempt them from the ranks of the suspects. Alas, they are as guilty as the rest of us. The scientist and the engineer are, after all, thoroughly human, and this means that they have aims to pursue and emotions to satisfy. Not only does the scientist want to discover new facts, he also wants to be rewarded for the discovery with respect, affection, fame, and money. To gain such rewards the scientist must persuade his colleagues, and society at large, that his discoveries are not only true (nothing is easier to make than a true discovery) but also important and valuable. And that's where the image-building comes in.

Having said this, I must nevertheless point out that not all professions and not all categories of writing are equally open to the same stylistic weaknesses. Scientific writing, in addition to being open to pomposity, wordiness, and hedging, is peculiarly vulnerable to a failing which yet remains to be discussed — the imitation of instruments and machines, notably those that digest and transform information. But scientific writing is not particularly open to flattery, except, of course, self-flattery; no writing is immune to that. This is because scientists, by and large, strive to impress other scientists and the layman not by flattering *them,* but rather by vying with each other in paying homage to their common deity — the Scientific Spirit. Fear of offending this awful Spirit may lead to such abject hedging as in the sentence about airborne sensors quoted in the last chapter. Businessmen, on the other hand, flatter one another; and the more remote their business is from the world of science the more they are tempted to resort to flattery to gain their ends.

This realization should help us to pinpoint the spots in the writing spectrum where flattery is most likely to occur. Such endeavors as personnel work, public relations, entertainment, politics are all heavily shot through with insincere protestations of sympathy, regret, affection, and respect. (I shall not concern myself with the language of commercial newspaper, magazine, or television advertisements. I doubt that the anonymous characters who concoct these effusions care a fig about manliness, precision, sincerity, or any other virtue, as long as they move merchandise.)

The real mecca of flattery, however, is the ladies' club. Women incline more toward fancy than toward fact — that, after all, is what makes them nice to come home to after a day of struggling with stubborn practicalities in shop or office. They have to watch more intangibles than men, and when they get together the effect is heightened several times over. Editors of women's pages all have stories to tell about the material brought in by publicity conveners and club secretaries.

The most easily spotted device of the flatterer is capitalization. The use of capital letters in the English language has steadily shrunk from its high point in the late Middle Ages, when English had as many capitals as German. Capitals — or

The Mecca of flattery is the ladies' club

upper-case letters, as they are also called — are used now-adays for three purposes: to mark the beginnings of sentences, to distinguish the particular from the general, and to denote respect. There are also certain conventions about capitals in headlines and titles, such as the capitalization of all words but articles, prepositions, and conjunctions.

An illustration of the use of capitals for particularization is "democrat" and "Democrat." The first means any person of democratic convictions, and the second means an adherent of the Democratic Party in the United States. It is easy to see that the capital is necessary here.

An example of respect is the capitalization of "Sir" in letters, as "Dear Sir." "Her Majesty" is always capitalized — which is more than loyal subjects would do a couple of centuries ago, when "her" or "his" was often spelled lower-case. The "President" of the United States, or any other nation, is usually capitalized, as are "Senators" and some other top-ranking political offices. But as we move down the line, capitalization becomes blurred, and rule of thumb, or flattery, take over. For example, it seems questionable whether the word "company" should be capitalized in the company's own literature, which also applies to the company's officials. One writer, showing unwise partiality, reported that "the conference was attended by both the president and the Chairman of the Board."

Personnel directors advertising for professional help often attempt to butter up prospective interviewees by capitalizing their degrees or titles. We find advertisements for "Mechanical Engineers," "Psychologists," and "University Graduates," as in the example cited in Chapter 2. Since these advertisements deal with general terms rather than particular offices, flattery is the only explanation.

But, as I said earlier, it is the club, and especially the ladies' club, which pulls all stops on flattery and therefore on capitals. Not only are the various offices in the club hierarchy capitalized almost as a matter of routine — Treasurer, Secretary, Program Chairman, etc. — but all committees, subcommittees, and activities as well. We read of the "Membership Drive" and the "Annual Spring Dance," we learn that "three Guests were present at the last Regular Meeting," and that "the Church Supper was followed by Choral Singing."

Such excessive use of capital letters is a bit ludicrous, and it can also be confusing, as when we read in a program:

Mrs. J. Mortimer Katz, the noted authority on Domestic Pets, who your Program Committee has been fortunate to secure for our Lecturer next Thursday Nite, will discuss her new book on the Early History of Cats.

Chairman Of The Board and president

Enthusiastic club members who might rush out to secure this fascinating volume would find to their chagrin that the book-stores were ignorant of it. No wonder: the real title of the book is "Felines and Pharaohs," and the club circular has wrongly capitalized a general description of it.

The best general rule on capitalization is — when in doubt, don't. You may be wrong now and then, but the chances of being wrong are considerably less than if you follow the opposite maxim.

Flattery, of course, has more extensive ramifications than capitalization. Among these are the insincere compliment and the insincere expression of regret.

The former is evident in this quotation from a textbook for supervisors, or what is sometimes described as "lower-echelon administrative personnel":

The supervisor is perhaps the most important person in any organization, whether it be a government department, an industrial plant, a business office or a religious order.

Surely any organization in which supervisors are more important than the general manager is sick, and any supervisor worth his salt will see this. The only effect such a sugar-coated statement can have is to engender doubts about the honesty of the rest of the text.

Goodness knows that a bit of insincerity is essential in social intercourse, and the white lie is one of the factors that make civilization possible. But we must be careful lest our

It is regretted that we cannot offer you a position at this time

insincerity do more harm than good. This is particularly true of insincere regret. Here is a good example:

While we have been impressed with your extensive qualifications and experience, we regret that we cannot offer you a position at this time.

This sentence obviously implies that at some other time the company may well have an opening for the recipient of the letter. If he is smart, however, he will not hold his breath while waiting for it. Such phrasing generally betokens nothing more than a bit of cowardice on the part of the writer who is unwilling to assume complete responsibility for an unpleasant decision and seeks to imply that the recipient is the victim of unfavorable circumstances. In the same category is the letter which says:

Although your research project clearly has merit, it is regretted that the Foundation cannot grant you the sum you request in this instance.

Here again the anxious researcher, looking for some silver lining, may be pardoned if he concludes that he may yet succeed in prying some money out of the foundation if he waits a bit, rewrites his application, and enters a lower amount. Chances are that he is in for a disappointment.

Sometimes letter writers try to dissociate themselves from disagreeable news by passive sentence structure:

Dear Sir: It is extremely regretted that due to a shortage of married quarters you are hereby notified that you must vacate your quarters.

Whenever we seek to shift the burden of an unpopular decision from our own shoulders onto the force of circumstances, we must be prepared to revoke that decision should the circumstances change. Conversely, every compliment implies a promise of support: people are expected to go to bat for the things they cherish. A German proverb says that he who says A must also say B — meaning, in this case, that one insincere statement usually involves the writer in another insincere statement, whereby he has to weasel out of a commitment he should never have made in the first place.

8
Missing Link

I SAID at the beginning of this book that I did not intend
to dwell on grammar, because with most writers grammar
was not much of a problem. In this chapter I may seem to
deviate from that program, but the deviation is more apparent
than real. The reason is that the fault I am going to describe
has become so prevalent and typical among modern writers
that it can no longer be ascribed to poor grammar alone but
must be regarded also as an expression of personality.

What I am referring to is the hyphen, or, more exactly,
the omission of it.

You may be surprised that I should devote a whole chapter
to so insignificant a sign, which has often been treated with
humorous deprecation rather than respect. But I think you will
agree after you read these pages that the omission of the hyphen
is nearly as bad a fault as hedging or wordiness.

The English language, though it generally follows the
Germanic languages in its structure, inclines toward the Latin
ones in its resistance to compounding. While the Germans
write "Haustür," the English write "house door" and the
Spanish "puerta de la casa." Now it would not be strictly wrong
to write "house-door" and make the hyphen do for us what
the compounding into one word does for German and the

more roundabout "de la" does for Spanish, but it is not normally necessary.

There are, however, numerous compounds of two, three, or more words in English where the hyphen is essential.

It was in 18 . . that the first iron ore carriers made their appearance on the Great Lakes.

The resistance of English to compounding

As the sentence stands, it can mean only one thing — the appearance of iron ships for carrying ore, any kind of ore. Should we wish to refer to carriers of iron ore, we would have to hyphenate — "iron-ore carriers."

The omission of the hyphen has become almost standardized in such expressions as "this store is air conditioned," "he is a data processing technician," "she is working in a real estate office." Taken quite literally, the second of these examples means that "he is a data, processing technician"; the third example means that "she is working in a genuine estate office." The compounds, of course, should be hyphenated — "air-conditioned," "data-processing," "real-estate." The trouble with these and similar compound adjectives is that in different contexts they may not be compounds at all, but adjective and noun. We can, for instance, say that a man "sells real estate," where "real" modifies "estate," whereas in the earlier example "real-estate" modifies "office."

Before you get discouraged by these technicalities, let me assure you that you do not need to analyze your sentences by parts of speech in order to become an expert hyphenator. Since by far the most common hyphenated compounds are adjectives, there is a simple rule of thumb which works in most cases. It goes as follows: If you have two or more modifiers preceding a noun, check each of them against the noun and see whether it gives the noun an appropriate meaning. For example:

This is a good looking girl.

We check and see whether "good" and "looking" apply separately to the noun "girl." Is she good? Is she looking? If *either* is inapplicable, then the modifier must be hyphenated — "good-looking."

Or again:

Jack is building a two car garage.

It may be a "car garage," but is it a "two garage"? No. It is plain that "two-car" must be hyphenated.

The same applies to three or more modifiers. Let's take this rambling but by no means atypical sentence:

The company specializes in the production of heavy large caliber medium to long range half track equipped field guns.

Only "heavy" and "field" can be applied independently to "guns." We can, of course, also speak of "half-track guns,"

A good looking girl

but this modifier has already been captured by "equipped," which is completely inapplicable by itself, as are "caliber" and "range." With the hyphens in their proper places, the sentence therefore looks as follows:

The company specializes in the production of heavy large-caliber medium-to-long-range half-track-equipped field guns.

Instead of eleven apparent modifiers we now have five, each of them a bona-fide adjective that has an intelligible meaning when applied separately to "guns."

Not all missing hyphens can be so easily inserted by an outsider. In many cases only the writer himself could know whether two or more words represent a compound or not. If he fails in his duty, he carries his secret to the grave — and with it the meaning of his message. If he speaks about "hot rolled steel coming off the production line," we quite naturally conclude that he is referring to hot steel that has just been rolled. He may, however, also have meant steel that was rolled hot rather than cold, in other words, steel that was "hot-rolled" rather than "cold-rolled," — two different methods of rolling. But if there are no other clues in the story, we cannot know this.

How prevalent is the omission of the hyphen? Out of curiosity I counted the number of missing hyphens in a 7,600-word article on steel production I just edited. It came to 226, or about seven missing hyphens per typewritten page. This, I believe, is about par for the course, at least as far as metallurgical literature is concerned. A dull headache is the least of the evils caused by the reading of such writing.

Some writers, having abandoned hyphens, nevertheless feel vaguely disturbed by the disconnected and almost incomprehensible staccato of modifiers clattering from their typewriters. To assuage their guilt feelings, they begin to set off their un-hyphenated compounds by commas, which in this case is not only unnecessary but ungrammatical. Thus, in our example about the field guns, they would write "heavy, large caliber, medium to long range," etc. Two wrongs, as the saying goes, do not make one right.

You may say, "All right, those sentences do become clearer with the proper placement of hyphens — but aren't they pretty awkward nonetheless?"

Of course they are. And here we have touched the twin demons that drive the pompous, unsure writer to do two oddly contradictory things: to frame his sentences in such a way as to form a great many multi-word compounds, and to drop the hyphens which alone can make these compounds intelligible.

The first of these two demons is the computer syndrome, for which I have reserved a later chapter. The second demon is our old acquaintance from Chapter 4, pomposity in the shape of noun-addiction.

Let us look once more at the first example of this chapter, the "iron ore carrier." As it stands, this expression is particularly satisfying to the pompous writer, because it consists (or *seems* to consist) of three solid nouns, three big words. Make it "iron-ore carrier" — if that is what it should be — and what have you got? Only one noun and one adjective. You have, in the pompous writer's view, with one tiny stroke of the pen scuttled two perfectly good image builders. Is it any wonder that he recoils from such deeds?

Therefore he dotes on sentences such as the following:

The reduction process gases are pressure exhausted up two 187 feet by 5 feet inside diameter stacks.

This statement, which attacks our brain with the rat-tat-tat of red-hot rivets, seems to contain no fewer than eight nouns. When we insert the proper hyphens, we get:

The reduction-process gases are pressure-exhausted up two 187-feet-by-5-feet-inside-diameter stacks.

This leaves us with two nouns, "gases" and "stacks." It also leaves us with an awful-looking sentence as well as an almost meaningless compound adjective. It is obvious that the whole "187-feet . . . diameter" modifies "stacks." But inside this monstrous adjective there is hidden a noun with its very own modifier — the "5-feet inside diameter." Obviously "187 feet" does not apply to the diameter; that, we guess, is the *height* of the stacks. Yet we cannot possibly split up that long compound into two — what will become of "by"? No matter how we look at it, the sentence is gobbledygook. It cannot be rescued by hyphenation; it can be redeemed only by rewriting, roughly along the following lines:

The gases from the reduction process are exhausted, through pressure, by being passed up two stacks with an inside diameter of five feet and a height of 187 feet.

One thing at least is clear — brevity is not synonymous with clarity.

If all this has left you with an antipathy toward hyphenated compounds, that may not be so bad. It may help you to avoid the excesses in compounding found in much of today's technical and scientific literature. You will not be able to avoid them all, of course, and in moderation they can be quite useful. Many have become so much part of our everyday language that we cannot write about many subjects without using them.

Whatever the merits of the hyphenated compound, the

A compound found snaking like a Chinese dragon through an article on tourism

omission of the hyphen itself is a sign, among other things, of pomposity, since it tends to clutter up the language with extra nouns. It is, of course, also ungrammatical.

For a parting shot, let me cite what I believe must be the granddaddy of all compound adjectives. It was found snaking like a Chinese dragon through an article on tourism:

> *One reason responsible for the increased travel by Americans abroad to Europe is the new policy of many air lines whereby immediate passage is available on a 10-per-cent-down-and-twelve-months-in-which-to-pay-remainder-of-cost-of-ticket plan.*

Only seven of the compound's sixteen words were hyphenated in the article itself. Either the writer faltered in his bold resolve to create the most preposterous word in the English language, or the linotype operator ran out of hyphen matrices.

9

Action, Please!

I SAID earlier that simplicity is the foundation of good writing, and that the failings I was about to describe were not learned in school but later in life. In the meantime we have been busily taking apart and simplifying inflated and corrupted prose; in other words, we have been reversing the chronological process. Now criticism is a particularly satisfying endeavor — for the critic, that is; but it does have this negative, reverse tendency, which makes it difficult for us to put ourselves in the place of the character who is being criticized. And unless we do this we shall never truly understand and get rid of the failings that are the subject of this book.

In this chapter we shall therefore try to unravel the tangled skein of bad style from the other end, and follow a piece of writing through several stages, from its simple, straightforward origin to its inflated, insincere apotheosis. Like most such models, this one suffers from artificiality. The human psyche does not work quite in this mechanical fashion, and of course the brain is lightning-quick and accomplishes in instants what is here spread out over several pages.

With this caveat in mind, let us look in on Robert F. Norris, Ph.D., a division head in a geological research organization. Dr. Norris is about to compose a letter to a subordinate, Dr. Watkins. Dr. Watkins, aged 62 and fifteen years Dr. Norris's

Following a piece of writing from its straightforward origin to its inflated apotheosis

senior, is working on a project in the division's laboratory. The division is planning to mount a research expedition to Baffin Island, situated off Canada's north coast and somewhat larger than California. The aim of the expedition is to make a series of relatively simple, standard observations at many widely dispersed points. This means that the members of the expedition need not have a great deal of scientific knowledge, but they must be physically fit, agile, and co-operative.

Dr. Norris's problem is this: Dr. Watkins has expressed a desire to go along with the expedition. For many years he has nursed a pet theory about certain phenomena on Baffin Island which he would dearly like to verify, and this may be his last opportunity to do so. Unfortunately, there are several reasons against including him. He is in good health and is known to take long, solitary walks through the surrounding hills, but he can obviously not be expected to work as hard and travel as much as the younger members of the team. His pet theory is considered just that by most colleagues, including Dr. Norris, and its verification barely seems to justify the probable expense. But what is more weighty yet is Dr. Watkins's difficult temperament. He is opinionated, reserved to the point of arrogance, and, being a bachelor, has developed a fixed set of habits and predilections that cannot fail to clash with the casual, improvisatory ways of an expedition. The other members of the team, mostly youngish men still working toward their Ph.D.'s, contemplate the prospect of having Dr. Watkins along with feelings just short of horror. On the other hand, Dr. Watkins is an able and dedicated scientist who has contributed a good deal to the organization, and he is getting along fine in the laboratory where he is able to work mostly by himself.

Dr. Norris has threshed all this out with the man who conceived the expedition in the first place, Dr. W. C. R. Gardner, the organization's director of Arctic geology, and both have concluded that Dr. Watkins cannot go.

Here, then, is the first version of the letter that forms itself in Dr. Norris's mind. It is a basic letter, if you like, neither particularly good nor bad, the sort of thing a man might write on the spur of the moment did he not have to watch out for and placate the demons of pomposity, wordiness, hedging, and hypocrisy.

Dear Dr. Watkins:

When we discussed the Baffin Island trip three weeks ago, I told you that the terrain to be explored was extremely rugged and that I was looking for younger men who would not mind the hardships. Also, the observations to be made are relatively simple and quite within the capacity of less experienced colleagues.

I have, therefore, reluctantly decided to decline your
generous offer to go along. I am sure you will under-
stand the need for this decision, which has been approved
by Dr. Gardner.

I am glad to hear that your current research project
is coming along well, and I shall not hesitate to recom-
mend that it be continued next year.

Yours sincerely, etc.

One thing that stands out about this letter is that it is less
than frank. I said earlier that white lies help to make civilization possible, and it would have done no good and probably
much harm had Dr. Norris been blunt about the reasons for
rejecting Dr. Watkins. There are other points: The first few
sentences repeat what is almost certainly known to Dr
Watkins; "I am sure you will understand" really means "I hope
you will understand"; and the last paragraph might not have
been added, had it not been for the disappointing news in the
other paragraphs. Nonetheless, these are hardly things to
cavil about.

This letter, of course, never gets written. Even as its dim
outlines begin to form themselves in Dr. Norris's mind, his ego
takes charge and proceeds to build up his image, by adding
nouns and important-looking words. To help you identify the
additions and changes, the key words have been underlined

Dear Dr. Watkins:

You may recall that when the subject of the Baffin
Island Expedition was under discussion three weeks ago,
I made mention of the fact that the terrain slated for
exploration was characterized by extreme ruggedness, and
that for reasons such as this I was considering younger
men who would not object to the hardships. As well,
the observations involved are of a relatively simple

nature and quite within the capaciti_es_ of colleagues with a lesser _degree of experience._

I have therefore decided, _with reluctance,_ to decline your generous offer to _participate in the Expedition._ I am sure that the _necessity_ for this decision will _meet with your understanding._ I might add that my decision has the _full concurrence_ of Dr. _W. C. R._ Gardner.

It has given me great _pleasure_ to hear that the _Research Project_ in which you are currently _engaged_ is

Dr. Norris's inflated ego takes over

progressing favorably, and I shall have no <u>hesitation</u> in
forwarding a recommendation for its <u>continuance</u> in the
<u>coming</u> year.

Yours sincerely, etc.

Apart from the extra nouns and the use of "big" words such
as "involved," "participate," "engaged," etc., I might point to
the opening ("You may recall") which suggests that Dr. Norris
himself may have had some difficulty recalling a conversation
which is only one of many he has held in his busy and
important life. This, of course, is nonsense; and it may be
assumed that Dr. Watkins himself has been thinking of little
else. Pomposity is also served by the capitalization of "Expedition," and a weak attempt is made to butter up Dr. Watkins
by capitalizing "Research Project."

Dr. Norris's ego is now satisfied with his image. But apprehension sets in: the letter places responsibility far too obviously
on Dr. Norris's shoulders. Also, that direct promise about
personal support for Dr. Watkins's research project will have
to be watered down. The new version of the letter therefore
reads as follows:

Dear Dr. Watkins:

You may recall that when the subject of the Baffin
Island Expedition was under discussion three weeks ago,
mention <u>was made</u> of the fact that the terrain slated for
exploration was characterized by extreme ruggedness and
that for reasons such as this <u>it</u> had been decided that
consideration <u>be given</u> to younger men who would not
object to the hardships. As well, the observations involved
are of a relatively simple nature and quite within the
capacities of colleagues with a lesser degree of experience.

The decision <u>has</u> therefore <u>been made</u>, with reluctance,
to decline your generous offer to participate in the
Expedition. <u>It is</u> hoped that the necessity for this decision

will meet with your understanding. I might add that
the decision has the full concurrence of Dr. W. C. R.
Gardner.

   It has given us great pleasure to hear that the Research
Project in which you are currently engaged is progressing
favorably, and there is every reason to anticipate that
a recommendation for its continuance in the coming
year will be forthcoming.

Yours sincerely, etc.

Note how Dr. Norris's personal involvement is played down
to the point of self-effacement. Will this fool Dr. Watkins?
Hardly. *He* knows who has made, and will make, the decisions
affecting his work.

But Dr. Norris is not yet satisfied with these cautious amend-
ments. He has, after all, not only Dr. Watkins to think about.
A carbon copy of the letter will go to Dr. Gardner, and the ·

He plays down his personal involvement to the point of self-effacement

file will probably pass through several other hands. There are also the various clerks and other minor office types who may read and, in their limited wisdom, misconstrue the meaning of this or that phrase. It is therefore necessary to make the meaning of each sentence proof against quibbling or tampering, in and out of context. That is where the letter becomes wordy.

Dear Dr. Watkins:

You may recall that when the subject of the forth-coming Baffin Island Expedition was under discussion three weeks ago, at the beginning of February, mention was made of the fact that the terrain slated for exploration was characterized generally by extreme ruggedness and that for reasons such as this it had been decided that in the selection of Expedition personnel consideration be given chiefly to younger men who would not object to the very real hardships involved in the exploration. In addition to the foregoing, the observations involved are of a relatively simple nature and quite within the capacities of colleagues with a lesser degree of experience than that possessed by older scientific personnel.

The decision has therefore been made, although with reluctance, to decline your generous offer to participate in the Baffin Island Expedition. It is hoped that the necessity of confining the Expedition to relatively younger men which formed the basis of this decision will meet with your understanding. I might also add that this case has been thoroughly reviewed by the Director of Arctic Geology Dr. W. C. R. Gardner, and the decision adopted has his full and complete concurrence.

It has given us great pleasure to hear that the Research Project in which you and your staff are currently engaged is progressing favorably to date, and there is

every reason to anticipate that a recommendation for its
continuance in the coming year will be forthcoming <u>at</u>
<u>the appropriate time</u>.

Yours sincerely, etc.

The additions in this version explain themselves. It is merely worth noting that the over-cautious, legalistic language which the last paragraph has now assumed is sure to destroy whatever beneficial effect it may have had at the beginning.

Dr. Norris's ego is now satisfied with the letter as far as image and security are concerned. But it cannot be denied that the letter does lack warmth. Dr. Norris therefore strives to add this desirable quality, but even with the best intentions he can hardly have much success.

Dear Dr. Watkins:

You may recall that when the subject of the forthcoming Baffin Island Expedition was under discussion three weeks ago, at the beginning of February, mention was made of the fact that the terrain slated for exploration was characterized generally by extreme ruggedness and that for reasons such as this it had been decided that in the selection of Expedition personnel consideration be given chiefly to younger men who would not object to the very real hardships involved in the exploration. In addition, <u>as you are no doubt aware</u>, the observations involved are of a relatively simple nature and quite within the capacities of colleagues with a lesser degree of experience than that possessed by older, <u>more highly trained</u> scientific personnel.

The decision has therefore been made, although with <u>extreme</u> reluctance, to decline your generous offer to participate in the Baffin Island Expedition. It is hoped that the necessity of confining the Expedition to relatively

*younger men which formed the basis of this <u>unavoidable</u>
decision will meet with your understanding and <u>apprecia-
tion</u>. I might also add that the case has been thoroughly
and <u>sympathetically</u> reviewed by the Director of Arctic
Geology, Dr. W. C. R. Gardner, and the decision adopted
has his full and complete concurrence.*

*It has given us great pleasure, <u>believe me</u>, to hear that
the Research Project in which you and your staff are
currently engaged is progressing <u>very</u> favorably to date,
and there is every reason to anticipate that a recommendation for its continuance in the coming year will be
forthcoming at the appropriate time. <u>If I can be of service
to you again, please do not hesitate to communicate
with me</u>.*

Yours sincerely, etc.

This is friendliness? Alas, no. It's an insult, and that last
sentence is the final straw.

Yet this is the only version of the letter that actually gets
written and that goes out in the mail to Dr. Watkins.

For the statistically minded we might note that whereas
the percentage of nouns in the first version was 11, in the
final version it has risen to 21. In other words, though the
length of the letter has about doubled, the number of nouns
has almost quadrupled.

Do you despise Dr. Norris? Don't. He is really a nice fellow.
He has opened his hospitable home to numerous visiting scientists, is a well-liked member of two clubs, kind to children
and animals, and ten years ago he risked his life by jumping
in between the ice floes to save a careless student-helper from
drowning. It is just that when he sits down to write or dictate
a letter something happens . . .

There are Dr. Norrises all around us; we meet them all the
time. More: there is a bit of Dr. Norris in ourselves. Unless
we recognize this we shall never improve our writing.

10

The Computer Syndrome

WE ALL need heroes to follow and, if possible, to imitate. As I suggested earlier, we tend to seek our modern heroes among the men with the white coats — the research scientist, the surgeon, the space explorer. But whom do these men and women themselves imitate? Their machines, that's whom. And since men are not, and were not meant to be, machines, a style that imitates machines derogates from our humanity.

The analysis of this trend is bound to involve us in somewhat more fundamental questions than our previous chapters, it may even get philosophical. But fear not — even if my statements may at times seem somewhat recondite, my examples are always down-to-earth. Put the two together, and you have the key for recognizing and improving bad style.

What is common to all machine data? Mathematics. Any computer expert will tell you that he can process or store any information that can be expressed in figures. And *only* that. Now what is it that sets mathematics apart from other types of "knowledge"? Timelessness. The truth of mathematics is outside time. We can envision worlds and ages in which everything is different from our own, except mathematics. Two and two must always be four, yesterday, today, and tomorrow. Mathematics changes not.

And, being itself changeless, it is ill suited to serve as a symbol for that which changes — life. From the unending stream, the ever-spiralling cycle of birth, life, and death, it snatches mere slices, slices which are still and lifeless. They may say: this was, then this, then this. But they cannot say: this turned into this which is turning into this and that. For mathematics there is only being, not becoming.

But language, being a mirror of man's experience, must itself re-enact experience if it is to have a human meaning. Consider this simple sentence:

This house has three stories.

This is a re-enactment, a representation, of experience. First we see the house as a house. After we have identified it as a house, we perceive its qualities, including the quality of possessing three stories. And this, in turn, suggests something else: we ascribe to the house a quasi-human personality. It "has," it "owns," three stories. It is as if the house, at one time, did not have three stories and later acquired them, just as human beings are considered to acquire their qualities from their parents.

Let us now see how a writer afflicted with the computer syndrome would formulate this sentence. He would write:

This is a three-story house.

He would, of course, omit the hyphen. Do you notice the difference? There is complete, ahistorical awareness at once. It is all there, a group of data. Notice also that "has" has been replaced by "is," a much weaker verb. And if the data man could find a way of getting rid of it also, he would. The data man distrusts verbs — they suggest flux, action, becoming. They liquefy the narrative, and when he reaches in to seize this or that phenomenon it slips through his fingers and rejoins the stream. He likes his data nicely frozen and separate, like ice cubes in the refrigerator. He is a great supporter of the true-false type of examination paper, in which students merely

A three story house

have to make a check mark or, better yet, punch a hole, because this kind of answer can easily be "quantified."

When such men write, even if their material is full of human interest, their prose has all the liveliness and color of a stock-market ticker. Here is an example, from a report on explosives:

Homemade bombs continue to attract young people, and three were killed in four incidents.

First of all, it is hardly the homemade bomb which attracts the young inventor; it is the *making* of a bomb in his home that attracts him. But to the statistical writer, the bomb *is;* it does not come into being. Even less satisfactory is the second half of the sentence. What does it mean? That three boys suffered a series of four accidents, whose cumulative effect proved fatal? Or some other combination of three and four? We cannot dare to guess. To tell *what* happened the writer would have to make clear *how* it happened. He would have to retell the happening itself, rather than flash before our mind a still picture of the result.

Here is another example, which is probably even more typical:

It is expected that cement manufacture will be a new industry in Smithville this year.

Does this mean that it was an *old* industry last year? That, at least, is what the sentence says if we take it at face value. To give it the sense the writer may have intended it would have to be re-phrased as follows:

It is expected that a new industry — cement manufacturing — will be established in Smithville this year.

This sentence accomplishes two things the other one fails to do: it shows that "new industry" is the general term, and that the particular "cement manufacturing" is included in it instead of being equal to it; and secondly, that it will *come into being*.

Writers who imitate computers shy away from spelling out actions and processes. If they are forced to connect cause and effect, they like to say merely that one is the result of the other:

A vigorous recruitment policy resulted in 40 per cent of the existing staff newly appointed during the twelve-month period.

The data man likes his images in frozen mathematics

Note how the verb "appointed" is buried in the middle of the sentence, far away from the cause, the "recruitment policy." This sentence is so badly mummified that it takes editorial expertise to breathe some life into it, together with some plastic surgery:

Thanks to vigorous recruitment, we were able to increase the staff by 66 per cent during the past year, so that two out of every five employees are new appointees.

I have, admittedly, taken some liberties with the original, but there are cases when this is justified. It was first necessary to give the percentage in terms of the starting point, not in terms of the result. In mathematics, 2 plus 2 is 4, but in life 2 and 2 becomes 4. Secondly, it is always helpful to give simple illustrations which can easily be visualized by the reader. This is especially important when one is writing about human beings.

Here are other examples of writing which give evidence of the computer syndrome:

Industrial assistance projects in Latin America included a variety of problems.

The projects hardly consisted of problems. What the writer probably meant was that the projects *dealt* with problems. The action is missing.

In the upswing of Canada's exports, dollar devaluation has been another influencing factor.

Once more we have the weak verb "to be" where we should have a much stronger one, viz., the upswing in Canada's exports was also "influenced" etc.

This is a potential oil and gas region.

Does this mean it is not an oil-and-gas region now? Clearly, to solve this puzzle we shall have to tell not what the region may *be* (data) but what it may *have* or *do* (action), i.e., that it may *contain* or *produce* oil and gas.

There is a developing doubt.

This is a pet phrase with many a producer of data-like writing, for whom things either are or are not. This is clearly a

There is a developing doubt

case where something is becoming, and the sentence ought to say, "Doubt is developing."

Where the little auxiliary verb "to be" does not usurp the place of another word, the other word is often cunningly misplaced so as to preserve the statistical effect:

The large percentage of time required for this program is because....

We feel that these are possibly premature requests.

I have not yet mentioned hyphenated compounds in this chapter, but it must be obvious that there is more than a casual connection between them and the computer syndrome. I suggested as much in the preceding chapter, and the very first example in this one shows how this connection comes about — the hyphenated adjective is often used to displace or weaken verbs. For flow it substitutes inertia. For example:

The ore concentrate is fed into 12-and/or-16-hearth roasting furnaces.

The "and/or" is unnecessary and confusing. The writer does not mean that there are furnaces having 12 plus 16 hearths. He means some have 12 and others may have 16 hearths, and the same roasting plant may use both models. But what we really want to get rid of is the cumbersome compound, thus:

The ore concentrate is fed into roasting furnaces having 12 or 16 hearths.

The same applies here:

During periods of low-to-moderate-velocity winds it is possible to travel down the lake for about 37 miles.

This becomes:

If the wind does not blow strongly it is possible etc.

The computer syndrome, however, is not confined merely to sentence structure. It has larger ramifications, but to unmask them would go beyond the scope of this chapter. The last chapter will have a few things to say on this score.

11

Whom Are You Trying to Impress?

MUSICAL PERFORMERS sometimes tell us — especially if they are the romantic type — that when they are faced with a large and oppressingly anonymous audience they pick out a pretty face in the crowd and perform just for her. This gives their music the intimate and distinctive quality it would otherwise lack.

Musicians, of course, are not the only ones who slant their performance toward certain persons while ostensibly performing for others. Historians have been known to write for their wives, poets for their mistresses, and scientists for their rivals.

Business executives, too, make a disguised pitch at third parties, mainly their bosses and secretaries. Few executives would openly admit that they stand in awe of their Girl Fridays, but many give themselves away. I knew one who was so afraid of his office helpmeet that he waited until she went on a six-week vacation to throw out useless old files which she had lovingly accumulated and protected over the years. As to the desire to please the boss, we need hardly expatiate on that.

These attitudes find their expression in style. Many businessmen fear their secretaries' ability to spell and pronounce better than they can, and therefore try to avoid words that might trip them up. To counter this they may try to impress their secretaries by dragging in needless technical details. They may grow uncomfortable and stiff in their language when dicating a letter to a female client or customer (the secretary might become jealous), and unduly reticent about their affairs in communications to their own lawyers and tax specialists (the secretary might blab). If they are better educated than their secretaries — this, too, is not infrequent — they may omit words and expressions which they fear their secretaries will not know how to spell or to punctuate. Being timid, they shirk their obligation to teach the girls.

Writing up to the boss is a familiar story. Organization men

Organization men sometimes use their correspondence to feed ideas to their bosses

who are aware that their bosses will, or may, read their letters and reports often develop a habit of feeding to them, in this roundabout way, complaints and ideas which they would either not dare to express face to face or which they believe would be fruitless if advanced directly. Let us say that 'Joe Smith, section head in a laboratory, would like to build up his staff. Whenever he receives a request for an urgent or complicated analysis he will slyly hint in his reply how the shortage of staff prevents him from dealing with the request as speedily as he would like. By and by Smith's staff shortage will crop up in correspondence all over the place, it will become a byword in and out of the organization, and sink quietly into the boss's consciousness. Unfortunately, it will also sink into the customers' consciousness, to the detriment of the organization — and Joe Smith.

Young professionals who may have eased their way through college by playing up to the opinions and preferences of their professors, often find it difficult to rid themselves of this habit of slanting their reports and memoranda to a father figure.

Other writers, particularly those in legal, financial, or government work, have a more abstract standard in their minds. They ask themselves not whether a letter or report will satisfy the boss but whether it satisfies the rules and regulations. Such pieces of writing often contain too little of what the recipient wants to know and too much of what he doesn't want to know.

Considering these circumstances, it is not surprising that so many letters, reports, learned papers, circulars, and what have you fail to do a good job. They carry far too much ballast, and badly stowed ballast at that.

The first requirement for every writer is to be himself. This does not mean that he must be an outsider, a lone wolf. To a large extent we are all products of our society. By being ourselves we cannot fail to give expression to such social influences, transformed by the prism of our personality.

The second requirement is that every writer try to fit his writing to his reader — not to third parties. This may not always be possible. You may not know your reader — his educational background, his exact needs, his character. Usually, however, you will have at least a general idea about the person or persons to whom or for whom you write. Not only the specific interests but also the tastes and intellectual levels of your readers vary greatly. It may well be that your writing is all intended for the same type of readership, in which case you can more or less follow a set stylistic formula. This, however, is exceptional. A consulting engineer, for example, who uses the same style in a report to the public-works department of a large city, staffed by fellow engineers, and in a report to a village council, composed of storekeepers, garage operators,

Some letters carry too much ballast

and plumbers, shows poor judgment. Millions of dollars in tax money have been wasted because contractors were too stuffy to explain to public bodies certain terms or conditions which would have been obvious to a professional.

The third requirement, of course, is to preserve the image of the organization or profession. While it is obvious that one should not use highly technical or elaborate language in explaining social welfare legislation to a slum dweller, it is equally true that we expect a certain dignity and reserve from certain persons. In a discussion of physical fitness, for example, the President of the United States and the high-school coach should not speak literally the same language. If they did, one would sound undignified and the other stilted.

I recall a corporation executive who prided himself on his ability to inject friendliness into his business dealings. He said that whenever he had to write to executives in other cities, even though he might not know them, he would start off his letter with a few casual remarks about his family, his dog, or the fine fishing he had enjoyed over the weekend. One may well wonder whether this sudden irruption of familiarity might not rather embarrass or annoy the recipient.

Similar to the presumption of familiarity is the annoying device of announcing certain assumptions about them to our correspondents. It is one thing to broadcast such assumptions to an anonymous, and probably unseen, readership, and another to thrust them at a person you are, so to speak, meeting face to face. Certainly you ought to form opinions about your correspondents, but be careful how you use them.

These psychological intrusions into letters are often joined by mechanical ones. Outstanding among them is the desire to put it on the record, if only for the sake of the file clerk. Here, for example, is the start of a letter from a government research agency to a mining company:

Referring to your communication of September 21 concerning a request of the Smith Asbestos Company Inc. to have tests made in this Department on samples from asbestos deposits in South Africa, I may say that our Mines Branch will be very glad to co-operate in this matter.

Of this whole complicated sentence, only the last portion belongs in the text of the letter. The rest is just so much deadwood, through which the recipient has to hack his way before he reaches fresh timber. But — the careful bureaucrat may object — if I omit these references, how will my correspondent, who is as busy as I am, remember what I am talking about? And, worse yet, how will my file clerk know under what head to file the letter?

Good questions. The most efficient system, it seems to me, is the old-fashioned *"Reference"* and *"Subject"* headings. These headings should be plainly separate from the text. The letter I quoted would then look like this:

> *Ref.: Your letter of Sept. 21*
> *Sub.: Tests on asbestos*

Dear Sir:

Our Mines Branch will be glad to co-operate on these tests.

Even more efficient is the coding of letters, coupled with a request that the correspondent repeat the code in *his* letters. This is done by a legend printed on your letterhead, saying: "In your answer please quote file . . . ." This will at least relieve your correspondent of the necessity of quoting reference and subject to you (provided, of course, he is smart enough to see this), and it will relieve you of the necessity of wading through them.

To some readers these systems may smack too much of bureaucracy. To the knowledgeable businessman or administrator, however, they are more likely to smack of efficiency,

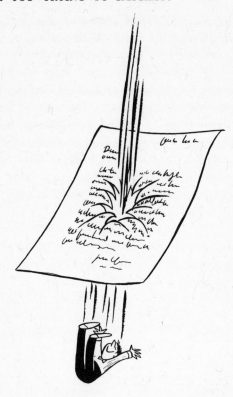

The thoughtful letter writer puts his correspondents quickly into the middle of the picture

because he will understand that they are meant to save him
time and effort.

Other readers may grant all this, and still be unconvinced.
They may feel vaguely uncomfortable about leaving out any
part of the story. What good, they may argue, is a cryptic
code reference to a previous letter if that letter cannot be
found in the files? They will want *all* the information in *every*
letter, even if this means transcribing (and reading!) the same
old phrases four or five times. Certainly, such practices do not
say much for these men's filing systems or their ability as
administrators. It's that old lack of confidence again.

These last few points may seem rather trite — after all, the devices I advocate have been used for centuries. But a quick survey of correspondence from the most diverse sources has convinced me that the mechanics of letter writing are in as poor a shape as ever, giving evidence of a widespread lack of elementary self-discipline.

Writing requires a good deal of imagination — no one will deny that. If you use some of that imagination to place yourself in your reader's chair, you may get an entirely new slant on your efforts at communication.

12

Planning Is Re-Creation

I SAID earlier that our writing should re-enact our expe-
riences, that it should follow the same path normally pursued
by our cognition. This, be it well noted, does not mean that
we must necessarily imitate natural processes themselves. What
goes on around us and the manner in which we learn or
experience it are two different things. It is almost a rule with
short-story writers *not* to start their story at the beginning,
for example, but to get the reader's attention with an inter-
esting event from the middle of the story, and then to take up
the beginning through a flashback. But even if they hint to
the reader *what* happened, they will take care not to reveal
how it happened. Suspense is as necessary to any good narrative, whether fictional or non-fictional, as it is to life. If we
knew at the beginning of our adulthood everything that was
to happen to us, life would not be worth living, for we would
be left without hope or ambition.

When I planned the book on the history of the Canada-
United States boundary which I mentioned earlier, I was pain-
fully aware that my readers would already know the outcome
of the various disputes. The boundary is, after all, a pretty
familiar feature; and in case readers did not have it present
in their minds I would have to remind them by including several maps.

Under the circumstances it seemed well-nigh impossible to build up any sort of suspense, i.e., a mood of wonder and expectation. Yet I have it on excellent authority that my narrative "retains a high sense of drama." I managed this by deciding from the start that I would refrain as best I could from telling the reader more than the characters in my story themselves knew at any particular stage of the history. Sometimes this took some sleight of hand, and I had to throw away some of the brilliant quips and scholarly allusions that are born of hindsight. But I am sure it was worth it. Although the reader has in his memory a clear picture of the outcome, his mind ignores it, as it were, and gets caught up in the development by assimilation.

This happens because our mind, given half a chance, will always choose flow and action in preference to static information. There is a saying that a picture is worth a thousand words. It is a proverb heard most often from people who have never really understood what writing is all about. The classical squelch is to ask them to show in a picture (or a thousand pictures) the dictum quoted earlier, "Do unto others as you would have others do unto you." It is a statement that demands an act of free will, and pictures or statistics cannot tell us anything about that.

I have earlier traced the connection between the mathematical "language" of statistics and computers, and the lifeless prose of their imitators. This applies not only to sentences but to the structure of the entire story, whatever form it may take — letter, essay, report, memorandum, or book.

Our life is suspended between birth and death, or, as the journalists put it, it stretches "from the cradle to the grave." Each sentence is, or ought to be, a tiny re-creation of that suspense between two poles. For example, a report compiled for a company producing ready-mixed concrete contained the following sentence:

Estimates of the reserves of sand and gravel in the three main gravel pits were made.

A sentence or a story is suspended between two poles

Even without analyzing this sentence we sense that it is awkward. The trouble is that the two chief elements of the sentence, the two poles between which it is suspended are the estimates and the three gravel pits. Between them should be strung the "life" of the sentence, the connecting action. If this is done, the sentence will read:

Estimates were made of the reserves of sand and gravel in the three main gravel pits.

Here is another example, from a fare schedule of a passenger line:

Children under one year pay a fare of $22. Children from one to twelve years of age pay half the adult fare.

The age of children on the day of sailing governs the fare to be paid.

The last sentence suffers from the same malady as the preceding example. It should read:

The fare to be paid is governed by the age of children on the day of sailing.

This places the chief element, the message, of the sentence where it belongs — at the end. "The day of sailing," that is what the reader wants to know next after having been told about the ages and fares. It may seem that these words should therefore follow as soon as possible after the second sentence; but the human mind does not proceed in this fashion. It has its own criterion; or, as the Greek philosopher said, "Man is the measure of all things." It is true that the sentence has had to be converted from the active to the passive voice, but that is the lesser evil.

What these examples illustrate is that it is not enough for a writer simply to divest himself of whatever information he has, no matter in what order or arrangement, as a tired man sheds his clothes before dropping into bed. He must, if you will pardon the simile, be something of a strip-tease artist, who knows not only *what* to take off, but *how* and *in what order*.

Writing demands rhythm, just as do music or dancing. It has been found, to the surprise of some historians, that the earliest literary compositions, recited by primitive men who could as yet neither read nor write, were usually in verse. Prose composition comes relatively late in the history of literature. To ancient men, who had to carry their literature in their heads, something as clumsy as prose simply did not seem worth remembering. Their standards were high, and they were not satisfied with beautiful content alone; they wanted beautiful form as well. Each piece of literature had to be as nearly perfect as man could make it. Hesiod, the great Greek poet, composed a long and often eminently practical treatise on agricultural pursuits entirely in verse; so did the Roman poet Virgil.

The modern junior executive may feel a bit uncomfortable at this intrusion of poetry into a textbook intended for his use. Mortally afraid of being considered an egghead or a long-hair,

Writing demands rhythm, like music or dancing

many an eager beaver in today's corporate world actually tries to write below his own taste or ability, preposterous as this may seem. He is under the mistaken impression (perhaps after reading the miserable prose of his superiors) that a crude, mechanistic style that clatters along like a worn-out dump truck marks the rugged, energetic comer.

But to get back to the question of rhythm in language. Here is the beginning of an article on women alcoholics in British Columbia:

A year ago one in every six alcoholics in British Columbia was a woman. Now more than 4,000 B.C. women — a ratio of one in five — are problem drinkers.

There is an evident dissonance between the two sentences (apart from the ungrammatical "one *in* every six"). Having put the stress on proportion in the first sentence, the writer shifts to number ("more than 4,000") in the second, burying the proportion in the middle. To harmonize these two sentences we shall have to make them read:

A year ago one of every six alcoholics in British Columbia was a woman. Now the ratio is one in five — more than 4,000 women with drinking problems.

What goes for sentences goes for chapters. Let us say that you are an executive in an automobile company, sales and service division, and that you have been asked to write a report on the operations of your dealers in five cities. Before you start your report you will have to sit down and figure out a plan — at least that is what you should do. You will be aware that there are several ways in which you can organize and combine your information. You can, for example, deal with the operations geographically, telling everything about the dealers in one city, then in another, and so forth. You can deal with the operations functionally, by telling first all about sales, perhaps make by make, and second all about service. You can combine the two methods, and tell first all about sales, city by city, then about service, city by city. Whether you adopt the first, second, third, or some other plan will depend mainly on what you are describing. If the operations are heavily influenced by geography, the strictly geographic approach may be best. If sales and service are governed by distinctly different sets of factors, the second approach may be best.

You might also consider whether to preface your detailed description with a concise summary for those of your colleagues who might not have the time, or the interest, to read the full report. Then again you may have been asked to make recommendations, and you will have to decide whether to append

Good writing unfolds naturally, like a tree

them at the end of the report, or to embody them separately with your chapters or sections.

Whatever plan you adopt — for God's sake, stick with it.

My experience as editor has convinced me that failure to follow a plan is both more common and more obnoxious than all other structural faults combined. Yet when you come right down to it, it is nothing but lack of will power.

Suppose that you had decided to deal first with sales, city by city. Now sales obviously do have some connection with service, and in some cases this may be especially strong, as when a dealer's good sales record is being pulled down by poor service to new cars. If you lack self-control you may be tempted to drift from sales into service, so that when you come to the second portion of your report you have no coherent story left to tell. If this really bothered you, as it should, you could start a rescue operation by pulling service details out of the first section and transferring them to the second. This sort of thing, however, demands skill and effort, and is apt to turn out patchy. In some cases it might even be wise to chuck out your old plan and devise a new one, re-grouping your topics. One thing you should *not* rely on is the fond expectation that the various topics will fall into place naturally, that the story will "write itself."

This applies to headings as well. It is amazing how inconsistent even fairly experienced writers, such as research scientists, can be when it comes to dividing their books and articles by headings and sub-headings. They will use all upper-case letters for some chapter headings, and upper and lower case for others. Some headings they will underline, and some not. They will divide and sub-divide short chapters, for no good reason, and leave other chapters to ramble on for scores of pages, with nary a break.

When one tries to get some symmetry and consistency into this witches' brew, it often becomes quickly apparent that the organizational mess is merely a symptom of a deeper and much less easily cured malady: the writer has no firm conception of values concerning his own material. He is not sure about what is important and deserves a chapter of its own, and what can be dismissed in a few paragraphs. Instead of his dominating the material, the material dominates him. It runs away with him.

This cannot be corrected by chopping up a manuscript into sections of, say, ten or twenty pages each and calling them chapters. Structure cannot be imposed on a manuscript that has no internal structure to begin with, any more than one can put together a living tree out of an assortment of roots, branches, and leaves.

And this brings us back to the process of writing as re-creation. The writer who wishes to explain something he knows must re-create, even if only in a summary fashion, his own process of understanding so that the reader can understand with him. This may sound easier than it is — because for many people it poses a profound psychological problem.

I have sat opposite eminent experts, some of the most respected brains in this or that science or technique, and tried unsuccessfully to draw from them the material for an article or a press release about a facet of their work. It seemed quite impossible for them to communicate the story to me in such a way that I could master it in my own mind. Some of these men were sincerely puzzled and disturbed by this failure of communication, but others merely sat back with a smug smile as if to say, Well, it's not my fault if you feel like a fool — why do you go poking your nose into professional stuff that's way beyond you?

Yet I have wondered whether it is I who ought to feel inadequate. Behind that imposing posture, that air of tremendous maturity and expertise, I sensed a fear — a fear to be caught out in innocence.

We often hear it said of great thinkers and discoverers that they have about them "an air of wonder," "a childish innocence," "naïve curiosity," and so forth. What this means is that they have retained something from their childhood — a wide-eyed openness to the world. This takes a generous personality. To be willing to learn also means to be willing to make a fool of oneself occasionally. To explain something from the foundations means to return, as it were, to one's own foundations. It implies an admission that one was a child at one time, and quite likely a fool.

It is this that stops the insecure specialist or businessman from climbing off his pedestal. He is the man who knows what he knows and nothing more; who despises all youth, his own included; he is the Compleat Adult of whom people are apt to say, "I can't think of him as a child." When you meet such a man you can be fairly sure he is a poor writer.

In the prologue to Goethe's *Faust,* the producer demands

from the poet a play that will be "fresh and new, and both significant and pleasing"; and the jester adds, helpfully, that to write effectively is to write so as to inspire youth. He who is finished, he says, is impossible to please, but a person who is still growing and becoming is gratefully receptive. To which the poet replies: "Then give me back the days when I myself was still becoming!"

Happily, the exclamation is merely rhetorical: for the good writer, the days of youth are always here and now.